W9-CNA-954

# SENSE

# &

# NONSENSE

By

Don Morton Cornwell

7/99

Best wishes Maggie

# SENSE

## &

N
O
N
S
E
N
S
E

# THE POETRY OF DMC

Don Morton Cornwall

Copyright © 1995 Don M. Cornwell & Co., Inc.
All Rights Reserved

Library of Congress Catalog Card Number: 95-92251

ISBN 0-9646734-0-1

# Foreword

The fact that the *Nonsense* section of this book contains twice as many poems as the *Sense* section tells us something about the author. He has always been quick to detect parallels between rhyme and situations, or connections between words and sense. Or the lack of it.

When Joseph Epstein, the editor of *American Scholar*, recently dropped his bomb on today's poetry community in the form of an article titled, *Who Killed Poetry?* he was mourning the rhythm, rhyme, enjoyment and quotability he finds absent in much of the poetry currently being written. But either Don Cornwell has chosen to defy this engulfing trend on the part of his contemporaries or he disregards it completely as he continues to use poetry as a source of enjoyment for himself as he writes and for us as we read, letting his words dance for us and make us smile. Maybe even think.

- John Dickson -

# Acknowledgements

Acknowledgement is given to *The Chronicle of the Horse* for first publication of these poems: *Canine Grammarian, Shy Guy, Ungroomed, Under/Saddle, Moving Mountings.*

My thanks to Glenna Holloway, John Dickson and Tom Roby for reviewing the book and offering suggestions. If this be a silk purse, each of these friends be a bomyx mori.

The following poems were written for and dedicated to a person or persons:

*Lib*, For Elizabeth Kaitis
*Lizzie*, For Elizabeth McCosky, Sr.
*Grace for Heidi and Kyle*, For H. & K. Nieman
*My Only Love*, For Mary Kostka
*For Anne*, For Anne Corrado
*Matinée Idol*, For Joe Karmizan
*Elizabeth and Carl*, For E. & C. Hurst
*Lue*, For Lue Tracey
*Dad*, For Gusse Cornwell
*Mom*, For Emily Cornwell
*How do I Love U Diana?*, For Diana Mendoza
*Lord Leslie*, For Les Bright
*Daniel*, For Dan Hurst
*Brian's Psalm*, For Brian Elliott
*Shelley*, For Shelley Hurst
*Carl*, For Carl Hurst
*Marylyn*, For Marylyn Feder
*Bill*, For Bill Gapp

*To a Hot Dog Mom*, For Erwina Cornwell
*Different Kinds of Cats*, For Salli and Les Bright
*Jackson*, For Eleanor and James Jackson
*Chef Jackie*, For Jackie Marks
*Dear Elizabeth*, For Elizabeth Hurst
*José*, For José Mendoza
*Karen and Frank*, For Karen and Frank Corrado
*Lizzy McCosky*, For Elizabeth McCosky, Jr.
*Connie and Don*, For Connie Quaintance
*Christopher*, For Christopher Cornwell
*William*, For Bill Feder
*Kay and Bill*, For Kay and Bill Nebel

For Erwina

# TABLE OF CONTENTS

## PART I SENSE

## PART II NONSENSE

# PART I

# SENSE

# NEXT TIME

Come along young man.
Pick up your bat and glove.
Wipe those tears.
I know the Bulldogs won,
and that you, only you,
might have saved the game.
I'd like to say it doesn't matter,
but it does.
I'd like to say there'll be a next time,
but there won't,
not just like this.
But there will be other times
when a single hit will win the game.
You will get that hit, believe me,
next time.
I'd like to say I understand;
I don't, not enough.
Now come along and wipe those tears,
and I'll wipe mine.

# NIGHT OF THE FLIGHT

At ten the flame of lightning came,
  And the sky turned into day;
And hail beat on the windowpanes,
  And cast its icy spray.

The huge plane rocked and then it fell,
  And then it climbed again;
And then it fell, and then it climbed;
  And then began to spin.

The lights went out and engine noise
  Was hushed by rushing air.
The whistling sound warned of the ground;
  Or sea, if sea be there.

And then in space where nothing is,
  There was an eerie ring.
A starboard engine flashed with fire,
  And tumbled from the wing.

The screams of desperate fear began
  In bass and high pitched tones,
And all the screams were harmonies
  Of piercing shrills and groans....

*cont.*

Through clouds we slipped, then we dipped;
And pointed for the sea.
We bowed our heads, grabbed our knees;
And knew eternity....

We struck the sea at sonic speed;
Like a sharpened saber tool
That holds the angle divers keep,
Who do not splash the pool.

There was a splash, but was no crash,
No watery demise;
And then the nose was pointed up,
And we began to rise.

From depths of who knows just how far,
The plane swam for the air;
While not a sound was heard inside
Except the words of prayer.

We surfaced like a rocket shot,
Then fell back to the sea;
And gently then began to float,
Away from tragedy.

# NAUGHTY EYES

Please look at me again with naughty eyes
That hint of mischief known from other years
When hazel hues would twinkle in coy tears
And every glance you gave told tiny lies.
Look at me then look away.  Disguise
The glint and change the hint to timid fears
And coquet modesty, so it appears
You never really meant to compromise.
I watched excitement leave your eyes, replaced
By dignity, when surely both were made
As parts of harmony.  I've learned to know
Most beauty comes, the lurid and the chaste,
From sparks that eyes control; for faces fade
And gather lines, but age eyes never show.

# LIB

There's something regal in a quiet grace,
a bird in flight, a flower's giving birth to bloom.
There's something gentle in a helping hand:
a mother's touch, a teacher asking little minds to learn.

There's something godly in a thoughtful heart,
a friend, or one who could but won't forget.
Quiet grace, a helping hand, a thoughtful heart.
Each so much was Lib.

# LIZZIE

I walk the road from Slovan
In the quiet sound of rain,
As homeward bound from church I come
Through fields of golden grain.

For time is but a moment
When one looks back through the years,
And happiness remembers more
Than ever pain or tears.

At home there will be dinner
And that joyful giggling noise,
The kind you might expect to find
Where girls outnumber boys.

Then later on there will be chores,
The ones I do not mind,
To hoe the garden, work the soil,
And see my pets have dined.

This life for long will not remain
For some will fly the nest,
And Anna will be headed south
And Josie headed west.

And Mary will be gone a while
But then return to home,
While I will fall in love with Fred,
And lose my urge to roam.

*cont.*

Our family will start to grow
  With Fred and John and Liz,
And I will wish no more at all
  Except for life as is.

When after all the children grow
  So soon grandchildren come,
And Billy, Bruce and Brian
  May, perhaps, be names of some.

There also may be Judy
  And Patty close behind,
And just that they'll grow up too fast
  Is all I'll really mind.

When after all grandchildren grow,
  Then great-grandchildren come,
And Danny, Doug and Terry
  May, perhaps, be names of some.

There also may be Lizzie,
  And I'll guess not who's behind,
But just that they'll grow up too fast
  Is all I'll really mind.

I walk the road from Slovan
  In the quiet sound of rain,
And pictures of some bygone years
  Come back to me again.

# HIPPIECRITS

By chance I met a bearded lad
  Who wandered down our street.
His hair was at a shoulder length,
  And dirt had shod his feet.

He said the world's an awful place,
  A womb where war begins,
And man forgets in every fight
  That no one ever wins.

I tried to take an open view
  Of what he had to say,
But the stench of his aroma
  Soon sent me on my way.

He screamed I was a dirty pig,
  And yelled another name,
Which made me turn to face his wrath,
  And play his silly game.

I asked him if he meant the words
  About his hate for war,
Or was afraid to fight for things
  Great men had fought before.

I said that, yes, he'd almost fooled me
  With his long and stringy hair;
That he looked more like a female type,
  But what kind I could not swear.

*cont.*

I mentioned that the dirt he wore
  Was like that found on swine,
And not like grime young soldiers wear
  Who man the battle line.

I told him that his  filthy mouth
  Had made me sick inside,
But he, not I, was sick of mind
  If reason be the guide.

Then the error  of  my  judgement came
  And shed its light on me,
And gave me a perspective
  Where I could hardly see.

We spoke  from  different value points
  That  truly showed our age,
But who was in the right or wrong
  No one could justly gauge.

For we'd come from different countries
  Though our homelands were the same,
And never could we ever share
  The honor or the blame.

I'd  lived somewhere  in  terror
  In a land of want and need,
While the land he knew in childhood
  Was one of thoughtless greed.

*cont.*

I'd seldom known a moment
  Not a struggle to survive,
While he saw just  the poor and weak
  Who begged to stay alive.

Yes, our values varied widely;
  But in one thing he was right:
Our differences would not be solved
  By any kind of fight.

# WHY

Is not our love the perfect kind,
  Of which so few remain;
And only lacks the requisite
  Of shared and suffered pain?

Is ours not more a sacred  love
  That knows no jealousy
To spark the tongue in hateful words
  And nurture misery?

Is it not true all pressure swords
  Within their scabbards rest,
Not drawn for there's always been
  A plenty of the best?

Then why from every touch I give
  To which you don't reply,
Do I now know with certainty
  That you have said goodbye?

# GRACE FOR HEIDI AND KYLE

Thank you Lord for this feast,
  And joining with us while
We celebrate the wedding
  Of Heidi unto Kyle.

Bless this food, which you provide;
  May it nourish us,
And nourish more this marriage
  So grand and glorious.

Shower too your blessings
  On the life that lies ahead
For this precious couple
  In the years that they are wed.

May they not forget you Lord,
  And as you well know too;
While they want your blessings,
  What they need is you.

# MY ONLY LOVE

My name is Mary Agnes,
  And I'm 65 today;
Still cute and pert and saucy
  With something I must say.

So listen all my children
  While I speak a word or two
Of my very deepest feelings
  About every one of you.

First there were my parents
  And Joe and Anna too.
Within this tiny circle
  Was the only love I knew.

Then my dark and handsome Erwin
  Came and took me off one day,
And put me in his castle
  To live and work and play.

Though clouds sometimes hid sunshine,
  As often they will do,
Within this tiny circle
  Was the only love I knew.

*cont.*

We had a lovely daughter,
  But she stayed so short a while.
She left us for a boyfriend
  When such things were in style.

This gave to me a feeling
  That was mixed in point of view,
For within this tiny circle
  Was the only love I knew.

We were blessed with two more children
  From Erwina and from Don,
A tiny little princess
  And a brave Napoleon.

Christopher and Pipper
  Made their world debut,
And within this tiny circle
  Was the only love I knew.

Perhaps my needs are meager
  And I set my sights too low,
But this with  God beside me
  Is my only love to know.

## FOR ANNE

Happy birthday Anne.
  Come take a trip with me.
Not around the world again,
  But back through time to see,

Some of the memories we have shared,
  Precious to the mind
Picture thoughts of yesterdays
  That we left behind.

Nineteen thirty-seven was,
  Recall, the year we met.
The fall, the Chateau Ballroom, Anne
  I never will forget.

In nineteen forty, remember now;
  You and I were wed.
On the seventh of September
  Our solemn vows were said.

It was again September,
  The year was forty-two,
Frank was born, God's blessing,
  His gift to me and you.

*cont.*

17

And then in nineteen forty-four
  Another blessing came.
Paul was born in August
  To the Corrado name.

We bought the Garden Center
  In August forty-nine,
And then in nineteen fifty-two
  That home of yours and mine.

So swiftly then the years went by;
  For us four decades passed.
It was time to think of other things;
  To slow the pace at last.

In nineteen eighty, with regrets,
  And a thousand memories,
We sold the business and embarked
  To travel overseas.

Frank and Karen were doing well,
  With Kelli, Mike and Joe;
And Paul was helping Saudis out,
  This was the time to go.

To 75 dear years, dear Anne,
  At home on plane or ship.
Your life and loves have surely been
  Your very finest trip.

# MATINÉE IDOL

Joe began in movies,
  In a picture unnamed yet,
The marquee simply stated,
  *What you see is what you get.*

Next *Here comes the Bride*;
  Irene co-starred with Joe,
About a love and happiness,
  Which we, of course, well know.

*One Man's Family* was next;
  And Kay and Don we see.
Re-released, *Father Knows Best*,
  It's on late night TV.

*Anchors Away* told the tale
  Of a sailor far from home;
Who saw the world, won the war;
  And never more would roam.

Happy Birthday to you Joe;
  May we present this scroll,
For eighty years of stardom;
  Each an Oscar role.

## ELIZABETH AND CARL

And what is love without respect that pays
An ever growing compliment of worth;
Which says that one alone, a thousand ways,
Will be the salt and treasure of the earth?
And what is love if not a thoughtful mind;
Whose every care is for the other one,
Whose every act is born of being kind,
And nourished by no promise left undone?
And what is love if it cannot forgive
The error made on steps along the path,
And thus allow affection's seed to live
And bloom in absence from the seed of wrath?
Yes love, Elizabeth and Carl, is this;
But know: a sense of humor is its kiss.

# THE THIRD DAY

And so the earth brought forth in green array
A growth of plants and trees with fruit entwined,
Each one with seed according to its kind,
As night and morning came to the third day.
To man belonged the trees of fruit that they
Be food except, forbidden and enshrined,
One called the tree of knowledge of the mind,
Whose fruit would take all innocence away.
When now in pain and fear our lives begin,
And then by sweat of brow we earn our bread,
Who has not wished that life could be as sweet
As it was then before man tasted sin.
Our hope may be to know in years ahead,
What fruit it is of which we should not eat.

# L

How can one look back on fifty years
That were a sea of early dreams come true,
Through waves of worries that decades knew;
Before the calm had come to rest the fears?
And what of one who shared, and now endears,
A half a century of love that grew
Across a half a continent into
Memories that are the souvenirs?
Perhaps to view the years can be to say
Dreams come true for those who make them so,
And never wish their lives another way.
And to the one who shared is now to owe
The reason why today means more today
Than all the yesterdays there were to know.

# LUE

Lue was a friend of mine, and when I see
Her in my mind, I see a smiling face
Belying always any misery
That she might well have carried in its place.
Lue was a friend of yours, and though I may
Not know exactly why, I know you shared
My awe how she collected on her way
So large a cadre near who loved and cared.
Lue was a friend of ours. We can't forget
The tender ways that were her autograph;
Or know that ever more we're in her debt,
For all the happy times she made us laugh.
We miss and love you Lue, and bid adieu.
Our all too brief affair was knowing you.

# LAMENTATIONS

How solitary lies the city, once
So full of people.  Once among the brave
New nations, now become a widow; once
The queen of provinces, but now a slave.
How bitterly she weeps at night; the tears
Run down her cheeks; there is no one to ease
Her pain from all her lovers, friends and peers
Turned traitor and became her enemies.
What could she do but sigh and turn away?
Uncleanness clinging to her skirts had shown
She gave no thought her fate had gone astray.
Her fall was harsh, and she was all alone.
Look Lord, upon her misery.  Her sin
Was great, but also has thine anger been.

## MDCCLXXVI

How short, indeed, a memory has he
Who, at the tavern weekly over ale,
Spoke words of liberty in rapt detail,
And swore to fight to end the tyranny.
Where is he now? What newfound loyalty
Gives him belief an empire should prevail,
Which caused the strife to make his parents sail,
And seek a dream, now lost, of being free?
Yes, courage withers like the snow of spring,
And tavern words do not foretell a deed.
Ours is to know, a pain must be intense
To cause young men in fear to fight their king.
For them, like embers in the fire of need,
Let's fan the flame in words of *commonsense*.

# BAJA

Sun and sand and splendor, Baja by
The sea, with days of marlin pirouettes
And nights of clouds of stars.  A quiet place
For fishing, and a peaceful place for love,
Hidden from infrequent roads that roam
This paradise so many miles from home.
And shouting out their splendor, jewels above
The sand, the villas rise with gilded grace
To shelter every need, and one forgets,
Life is not real beneath the Baja sky.
Yet what may be in having once to see
This misplaced rose where only cactus grows,
Enlightens us enough to always own
A part of heaven few have ever known.

# NIGHT SHOW HOST

Some guest I've got!  How'd he make it big?
He's a nobody!
This guy made eleven mil last year;
doing nothing but insulting folks.
I'd like to say, "Hey stupid!"
But I never would,
'Cuz it's stupids just like him who make me rich.
There goes the camera, just on him again.
I'll bet he wants my job.
I think I'll ask him something tough, they'll see.
Why are they laughing?
Talent?  That's not talent!  Don't they see?
Why are they laughing?
He's just another unknown clown.
Thank God the show is almost over now.
I'll just go home and have a little cry.

# OTHER SIGHT

I never smelled the heather,
　Never heard the sea,
Never touched a flower
　Or saw one come to be.

　I know no taste of honey,
　My senses all are blind,
But God's whole world is shown me
　Through pictures in my mind.

# DAD

When I became a dad I hoped
The kind of dad I'd be,
Was like the dad my father was
To Connie and to me.
He treated us with great respect,
And placed in us his trust.
When we spoke, he listened,
What he spoke was just.
I seldom saw him angry,
Seldom heard him swear,
Rarely heard him gossip,
Or emanate despair.
When I was very certain
Of something that I knew,
He'd take and teach the other side,
The different point of view.
He seemed to have no problems,
Though this was wrong I know;
But his quiet calm in turmoil
Made us think it so.
Although a somewhat private man,
He was warm to all he knew;
A precious man and father,
Loved by us and you.

Gusse Harold Cornwell
Memorial Service February 8, 1986

29

# NOT TO KNOW

The cows were a mismatch of color
bumping each other at the gate
like a mannered crowd at the door of a wake.
It was milking time and they were anxious
to be milked and fed.

Only with the hours did discontentment begin.
Anxiety altered their lowing;
the bumping was hard and rough.
The usual tinkle of the cow bell
became as the clang of clapper,
and the pawing and fighting began.

Not one could see in the distance
that the house and the barn were gone,
nor know that their eyes now watered
from the smoke from the fire on the farm.

# END OF THE LINE

Hiss!      Sh!      Sh!    Sh! Sh! Shu!
Come on! Let's go, coughing iron horse!
The balm of life, that legacy of youth is waiting,
and I, unlike you with your huffs and puffs,
will move as do those cindered lilies
now running by the rails, their quiet hiding
the dirt upon each skirt.
If they live in such an unkind world, so can I,
and none will know mine is not the pure way.

*KEDZIE WILL BE NEXT! RURRrrrrrrrrr*

Diesel strength is wise, it works hard first,
then coasts along, and since all life is luck;
one must play the wheel of chance, and pray
that graying hair may still owe time for luck.
Those roses who bloomed late, knew victory;
though never quite so well who knew it young.

*GLEN ELLYN WILL BE NEXT!* RURRrrrrrrrr

A rocket train they say, I call it monorail,
My friends now ride in driver driven cars.
The last stop used to seem so far away.

*GENEVA! ARE YOU ALL RIGHT SIR?*

31

# INSPIRATION

Oh, Mary; let's not argue subjects now
that have been tender for a score of years.
The evening's late and I have much to do.
But briefly, yes, I know your life's been hard,
and now our Willie's gone, and you must feel
that I have also left your side. Yet I have
work in life you do not understand:
a nation's call to help someone in need,
the child of liberty, *equality*.
You may forget among your own concerns,
that war is here, and it will surely test
and tell if this great country can survive.
We owe much more than we can ever pay
to those brave boys who fought and died for us.
It was not meant that they should die in vain,
So we must see that freedom is reborn,
and not allowed to perish from the land.
The evening's late and I have things to do.
Our talk has brought some thoughts to mind
to ease my task. I'll jot them down tonight.
The trip tomorrow will give me time to hone
my words before I speak at Gettysburg.

## NO STRANGER

Come in quickly!  Let me close the door.
Surely fog and rain were never meant
to hide or injure such a pretty face.
My daughter is not home; but then, of course,
I did not ask; perhaps you're from the press.
Today was not to be a news event,
but rather just a gathering thanking those
who helped me reach some goals in politics
that prove you still can win with honesty.

You've such a pretty face and look so like
a girl I knew some thirty years ago.
We had a brief affair, I mean romance
but parted enemies.  She vowed revenge.
I married, yes, and then so strange is life
in later years I met her only child,
a girl; her twin, though not yet seventeen.
We knew each other well, I mean as friends
but parted enemies.  She vowed revenge.

I heard she had a child, but am not sure.
I only know one day she went away,
ungrateful for the year of help, when as
my aide, she seldom had to work at all.

*cont.*

33

Much like her mother was her every way:
Both talked too much and in the end with each,
I feared the things that they might say, all lies,
to hurt my wife, my bid in politics.
I think I feared that thing they called revenge.

Though why I tell you this, I do not know.
And yet your face reminds me, and you would
I'd guess, be just about the daughter's age.
Forgive the thought; she'd dare not come here
now.  Please dear, I'd like to have you meet my
wife. You two can chat before the guests arrive;
then you can meet my rumor thirsty guests;
who will be interested, I'm sure, if you have any
tales of gossip you can tell.

# MOM

My mother never yelled at me,
Except for once or twice.
Partly, this was just because,
She was so very nice.

Partly though, I aided her,
By also being nice;
But this is not to say at all,
We lived in paradise.

The worst thing that I often did
Involved a too-wet towel;
I'd throw it on some furniture,
And then my mom would howl.

Sometimes I'd start to tease my sis,
And mom would sure get mad.
When Connie threw some food at me,
I think that mom was glad.

Mostly mom would keep her cool,
Which can be hard with twins,
Like when they get in those bad fights
Where no one ever wins.

Mom found the time to cook for us;
We never missed a meal;
And when a wounded child came home,
She was there to heal.

# OH STAR !

Appear again most sacred star
In all your massive glory,
And light a path for His return;
Conclude the Christmas story.

# PART II

# NONSENSE

# THE SNOB AND THE SLOB

The guests seemed like a well-bred bunch;
  Except one gaunt and frail,
Whose quaint attire made clear the fact
  His school had not been Yale.
I watched him at his dinner seat,
  Aghast at what I saw.
He chose and used an inside fork
  Against all dining law.
Then next he reach with fork in hand
  And speared a shrimp of mine.
His arm came back and overturned
  A glass of vintage wine.
In place of an apology,
  The shrimp, now partly chewed,
He spit upon the damask cloth
  As he belched from other food.
When we adjourned to drink and chat,
  I watched what could not be;
The guests were talking to the slob,
  While no one talked to me.

# CANINE GRAMMARIAN

My dog knows English, one might say.
He's learned to lie down, not to lay.
He's found he's different from our cat;
Not different than, he'd not find that.

Some times he's wished he were like us,
Not wished he was, that's ludicrous.
He cringes when he hears "he don't."
He doesn't like it and he won't.

He's heard us talk of cat and he,
But knows that "him" fits properly.
He barks to say "May I go out?"
There's never "Can I?" in his shout.

He and myself - "myself, oh my!"
He'd frown because the word is "I."
Some say he's not "much of a pup."
He'd like to tell them, "Look that up."

# HOW DO I LOVE U DIANA?

How do I love U Diana?
Let me count  the ways.
I love you because you go all out,
Give one hundred percent, set your sights high,
And don't let grass grow under your feet.
You're a ball of fire, an eager beaver,
Always on the go, know the ropes,
Don't miss a trick, have a magic touch,
A heart of gold, call a spade a spade;
And in rough times, know which side your
Bread is buttered on. You swept me off my feet,
Knocked my socks off, and I went for you
Hook, line and sinker. I have to hand it to you,
You look like a million bucks, and I find myself
Sitting on top of the world.
I love you like it's going out of style.
Let's try for twenty-five, then more.

Ghost written for José Mendoza

# RESIGNATION

A boss and friend are hard to be,
  But you've been neither one to me.
The friendship lamp you never lit.
  And as a boss you're bad.  I quit.

# ASSUMPTIONS

I asked the banker for a loan.
He asked me for my name.
   "Cornwell," I said.
   "Cornwall," he wrote,
Which is really not the same.
   "First name?" he asked.
   "Don," I said.
   "Donald" he wrote down.
Although it seemed all right to him,
It was not the proper noun.
Yes, I got the money,
And I spent it on a spree.
And now the loan must be repaid
By someone who's not me.

# SEX PROBLEM

When I was learning grammar,
  It was clearly taught to me:
If sex is not explicit,
  Then the proper word is "he."
Today it must be "he" or "she,"
  Just "he" is thought absurd;
Because it shows a bias
  For a sexist word.
No longer can one ever do
  "His" very best to win.
Now it must be "his" or "her;"
  Or "their," a greater sin.
It all seems so ridiculous,
  And needlessly complex.
I much prefer what I first learned
  About the use of sex.

# SHY GUY

He did not like the tractor noise,
  And quickly stepped aside,
But sputter from a motorbike
  My horse took in his stride.

The open gate meant trouble near;
  He cocked his head and eyes,
But horrid trash beside the path
  Created no surprise.

A somewhat distant siren wailed;
  He missed an off side beat,
But closer rings of gunshot shells
  Did not disturb his feet.

Well that, of course, was yesterday,
  Which now has gone to ground.
Today his likes and hates may be
  The other way around.

# SILENCE

Your lips are wine.
  Your teeth are pearls.
The rest of you
  Is like most girls.

Press pearls in wine
  My little pup;
Which is to say, dear,
  "Please shut up!"

## HEAVENS ABOVE

So these are the pearly gates.
They are much as I imagined them.
Yes, I did live a good life;
  good to others and good to myself.
My philosophy was be nice to people;
  you never know when you may have
  a chance to take them for something.

*My name is Ashby, sir.*
Oh look! There's little Timmy Allen.
I remember when I stole and hid
  his new puppy.
He said he'd never forgive me.
I wonder if he did.

*My first name is John.*
And oh! There's Mary Jane.
I should have married her, I know.
I told her I would.
We sure had lots of fun for a while;
I'd rather not see her.
*It's John H. Ashby.*
And there's my boss, old J. C.
He didn't know what was going on.
I came in late and left early.
He never knew.
And when I borrowed from the till,
  he never knew.

*cont.*

*John H.Ashby III.*
And there's dear sweet mom.
I know I told her I'd write,
  and send her something now and then.
I meant to, but I was busy.
Moms understand that.

*John H. Ashby III from Clearwater.*
Oh, I see!
You want me to take
  the elevator on the left, and press
  *DOWN!*

# LORD LESLIE

Now hear this continuing story
  But in case you missed the first verse,
It's about our friend Lord Leslie,
  And his lady for better or worse.

It's the story that asks the question,
  Asked so often before
Can a girl from a caramel corn field,
  Find happiness once more,

As wife and loving mistress
  Of the richest and handsomest lord,
Or will she in future installments,
  Find herself totally bored?

As we open today's adventure
  We hear Lord Leslie say,
"Tomorrow is my fortieth birthday,
  And I'll want things done my way.

We'll arise, as usual quite early,
  So set the alarm for five;
We'll jog on the grounds for an hour or two,
  It's healthier than a drive.

Tell the Danish or Belgian servants,
  Or whomever we've got out there;
That I'd like spaghetti for breakfast,
  And be sure there's some sauce to spare.

*cont.*

49

After breakfast I'll build us a school house,
  I'll try to finish by ten;
So call up some kids to fill it,
  For I'll want to get started then.

At noon I think we'll go skiing,
  We all can eat on the plane.
We'll ski up the slopes, ride down the lifts,
  Then hurry back home again.

At three I've scheduled a hayride,
  So maybe your help you'd lend,
For I've got to plow the back forty,
  And I've also some fences to mend.

In the evening there should be a party,
  So invite a few dozen friends,
And we'll dance and revel together,
  Until finally this day ends.

Then we'll have a few moments together,
  And I'll prove I'm not over the hill.
So may I say, my dear in closing,
  Remember to take the...."

# UNGROOMED

She rang the stable to announce
She'd want her horse at ten.
The honeymoon had been great fun,
But oh! to ride again.

Arriving booted, dressed and capped,
She sensed a change in store
For things were clearly different there
From how they were before.

Her horse had not been readied yet,
Not brushed, not tacked, not tied
And when she found him in his stall,
A note was pinned outside.

It said that all the help was gone,
And she could now assume,
Although just wed, she'd henceforth be
A bride without a groom.

# IDIOSYNCRATICAL PROPENSITIES

Steak and popcorn salad
  With catsup splashed on grapes.
Spaghetti maraschino
  In vinaigretted crepes.

Chopped and pickled parsnips
  On a bed of licorice chips,
Served warm with honeyed oysters
  And some peanut butter dips.

Aspertamed anchovies
  With garlic cloves and cream,
On fudge and rutabaga goo;
  A fluffernutter dream.

Stew of tripe served à la mode
  To preview steak tartare;
A side of broccoli and sprouts,
  Also served quite rare.

A glass of wine with every course,
  Sometimes more than one;
A bunch of cordials later on
  When the meal is done.

Breakfast may be slim tomorrow,
  My wife gets home that night.
If I can make it one more day,
  Things will be all right.

# DANIEL

Hi Dan, my friend, how are things?
And how are you today?
This is grandpa calling you
From very far away.

Are all your trucks and cars O.K.,
And running well, I hope?
I heard that one had lost a wheel
Going down a slope.

And do you still go skiing down
That very super hill
Where you can not see the bottom
And you sometimes take a spill.

Well Dan, please do be careful now
And watch where you are going.
Yes, sometimes that is very hard,
Like when the sky starts snowing.

I hope that you are eating well
Good things like grapes and beans,
And getting some spaghetti when
Your plate is very clean.

Well Dan, I've got to leave you now,
We'll be talking soon again.
In the meantime treat your sister nice,
And Brown Bear too.  Amen.

# BRIAN'S PSALM

The Exchange is my shepherd,
  I shall not want.
It maketh me lay down my green money.
It leadeth me beside still open contracts.
It restoreth my position.
It leadeth me on the paths of great fortune
  in its name sake.
Yea though I walk through the valley
  of the shadow of the pit,
  I will fear no evil; for I art reckless.
My hedge and margin, they comfort me.
I preparest a table (point & figure)
  before me in the presence
  of mine traders,
  and anointest my portfolio with oil.
My cash runneth over.
Surely good luck shall follow me
  all the days of my life;
  and if I cover my options,
  I will dwell in the pit forever.

# LAND OF LITTLE LEAGUE

Some feel the awful wars we fight
  Begin upon the street.
Where poverty and property
  First have the chance to meet.

While this no doubt is partly true,
  Of similar intrigue,
Is how the seeds of war are sown
  In the Land of Little League.

Dinner must be served at five,
  Although we eat at six;
Then taxi service run to where
  They practice baseball tricks.

It's back to home to eat our meal,
  Then back to get the kids,
Then listen while the coach explains
  The wrongs that each kid did.

And strange it is of baseball folks
  Who notice every fault,
That they can't see the line of cars
  Which pray that practice halt.

And right it is about the boys
  Who come so far to play;
They truly are forgotten when
  It comes to big game day.

*cont.*

For  the  eager Little Leaguer from
  From much further down the road,
Soon finds he has a problem
  Because of his abode.

For even if he batted in
  That needed winning run,
It would be wished the score had come
  From the neighbor of someone.

You see the games they play each week
  Must cross the cocktail table,
And best it be a local kid
  Who gets the hero label.

So while it is, some people say,
  That war starts on the street,
Consider how it too might start
  Out where the baselines meet.

# FOLLOW THE DIRECTIONS

When last you asked directions
　To a place you had to find,
Did you not meet a friendly soul
　Trying to be kind?

Did he (or she) not give you
　A most assuring word?
"No problem" was the warm remark,
　That you clearly heard.

"Go up the hill and past the trees
　You'll see a flock of geese.
Go right, then left, then right again,
　Then down the road a piece."

So you took the hill, and past the trees,
　And saw a flock of geese;
Turned right and left and right ten miles,
　Then down the road a piece.

You did not find the place, of course,
　And your question then became,
Why, to every place there is,
　Are directions all the same?

# LIARS CONTEST

It was a bad year!

The spring was wet;
  so wet in fact,
it rained cats and dogs;
  who had kittens and puppies.

The summer was hot;
  so hot in fact,
the ill-behaved of Hades
  were sent here.

The fall was dry;
  so dry in fact,
the river ran to the ocean
  looking for a drink.

The winter was cold;
  so cold in fact,
night and time froze;
  and there was no tomorrow.

# SHELLEY

There is a girl named Shelley,
  Who lives so far away;
I seldom ever see her,
  We seldom ever play.

But when we are together
  I hear a roaring sound,
And think there is a lion
  As I see her paw the ground.

And then she gets herself dressed up
  In fancy clothes and pearls,
And makeup stuff of every kind
  Not found on little girls.

Then often she will call to me,
  She calls me, "Grandpa Don."
And if I don't come pretty quick,
  Miss Shelley will be gone.

I wish that she lived closer by
  So when she was a lion,
She'd  roar a lot, and never stop
  Until she had me cryin'.

## SORRY ABOUT YOUR FALL

The horse was unsurmountable.
Try something else, sir, mount a bull.

# RICH MAN POOR MAN

I bought a book called *Instant Wealth*,
   And put it to the test,
Invested every dime I had,
   And borrowed all the rest.

I put a hearty sum of cash
   In stock of Liquid Oil,
Then borrowed as much as allowed
   For a call on U.S. Coil.

The Dow went up; the market soared.
   My position grew secure.
I put a mortgage on the house,
   Bought tons of Always Pure.

Again I borrowed, and I bought;
   Again I tempted Hades.
My assets doubled, and not troubled
   I ordered a gray Mercedes.

Then in a place called Cameroon
   In a jute purse lived a weevil,
Though hard to conceive and hard to believe
   Caused a market upheaval.

*cont.*

A purse with a bug will not fetch a dime,
   In a country that has to sell jute;
So cotton can grow, and oil can flow
   And the country can live and bear fruit.

A purse with a bug meant very bad things
   To my precious Liquid Oil.
With a margin call, the same could be said
   Of my darlings Pure and Coil.

The book I bought, *Instant Wealth,*
   Proved true to its name, I guess.
But while wealthy I was for a happy short while,
   I was never spoiled by excess.

# LOVE OF ANOTHER KIND

He cantered down a winding path
  With dignity and class.
Then stumbled on a tulip stem,
  And left me in the grass.

He walked across a raging stream
  Without a trace of fear,
Then jump up halfway to the sky
  When a paper wrap blew near.

He trotted on, He trotted fast,
  He trotted off for home;
And I walked on, and I walked fast
  From the fence where I was thrown.

I love this horse, and used to think
  The horse also loved me.
But if he does, it surely is
  A strange affinity.

# THE ENGINEER

I built a better mousetrap
  So all the world could see,
How crowds of eager people
  Would beat a path to me.

Then I found and hired a salesman,
  So if my plans went wrong;
At least I'd have an order,
  Till the crowds would come along.

# CARL

My name is Carl, Carl's the name;
  I am an engineer.
I engine things and neer the rest,
  So all will well cohere.

My name is Carl, I mentioned that;
  I am on ski patrol.
It's a way to ski for free;
  It's how I pay the toll.

My name is Carl, a Norseman name,
  And often I camp out;
With Shelley, Dan, Hoback and Liz.
  Hoback's the dog, our scout.

My name is Carl from way out west;
  Cars and trucks my bag.
I find 'em, fix 'em up real good,
  And that is not to brag.

My name Carl, Denver Carl;
  Wind surfing is my game.
To get around, without gas,
  Has always been my aim.

# ANNIVERSARY

Thank you dear for many happy years.
Never once did you complain
  about running errands.
And thank you for the hours
  you  spent shopping with me,
  and for holding my packages.
And how wonderful it was
  you never did insist
  on entertaining "your" friends.
You never once objected
  to the clothes I bought on sale.
And how happy I am that you have left the
  decision-making to me.

Thank you dear for many happy years.
I have always marveled at your interest
  in rehashing a ball game, or golf shot.
Those many nights we spent in a sleeping
  bag on cold ground during a fishing trip.
The way you seemed to adapt;
  this showed you cared.
How well and often you laughed at my jokes
  or perhaps I should say, "my joke."
But most of all, thank you for not calling it
  to my attention when I forgot a birthday
  or an.... What's the date today?

# PROCRASTINATOR

This year I will get organized,
  And do each task on time.
I'll write the thank you notes I owe,
  To prove it wrong that I'm....
In spring I'll clean the house and yard,
  At least I'll clean the yard.
I'll plant my seeds in early May,
  At least I'll try quite hard.
In fall I'll rake the leaves before
  The winter's on the wing;
Or do it when I cut the lawn,
  Sometime in early spring.
I'll make my Christmas shopping trip
  Sooner by one day;
And not be out on Christmas Eve
  As was my former way.
This year will be much better,
  If I do what I have planned.
If not, I'll try again next year,
  And that year will be grand.

# A HUNTING YOU MUST GO

If you would be a gentleman
  Then ride sir to the hounds,
Where horse and grace and etiquette
  With money all abound.

To hunt is more to know the fox
  Than others in the cast;
For he, the cunning little beast,
  Lives just because he's fast.

Never will the fox be caught,
  But still the hunt goes on;
Waiting for that never day
  Of this phenomenon:

The master caped in coat of red,
  Described by lore as pink
Leads on the field, and whippers-in,
  And hounds with airs of stink.

Over the fence, across the field
  To grandmother's house we go.
To catch a fox and put him in a box
  And then to let him go.

*cont.*

So Tallyho, let's get the fox,
  Before he goes to ground;
And cut his mask as mark of kill,
  Then pass it all around.

But now my dear field master, sir;
  We huntsmen of good cheer;
Think its time to have a drink
  'Ere the fox appear.

So hold the horses, hold the hounds;
  A stirrup cup's my plea.
For the hunt is life at very best
  But the cup is ecstasy.

# MARYLYN

Did you know for a fact today turns the page
  To make Marylyn (hush), or close to that age.
I'd never have guessed it, she looks immature;
  I didn't say acts it, but looks it for sure.

She still is a beauty, a queen of the beach.
  While only concrete, it's beach to this peach.
But all who admire and love her, of course,
  Don't know these secrets from a close source.

She's known as the queen of the mini swim set,
  And she's also a queen to Charlie, her pet.
She's queen to her children, queen to her spouse
  Who'd surely agree as king of the house.

She's queen of the kitchen, providing for all,
  And queen as a hostess in her banquet hall.
They say that a queen's worth less than a king.
  Now that's a peculiar kind of a thing.

# THY NEIGHBOR

The guy next door won't cut his lawn,
  and leaves his garbage curbside week to week.
On the other side are kids who fight all day,
  and when they stop;
across the street a party starts with dolts
  who park their cars on our front lawn,
and smash their glasses in the street;
  while they sing college songs.
Then behind us are the quiet ones,
  who note each move we make;
but never speak a word.

A pity such a group surrounds our house,
  which boasts a dog that often doesn't bite,
a cat that entertains all night with song;
two kids who often don't throw beer cans
  on the nearby lawns;
and parents (us) that only in a most
  well meaning way,
suggest just how each neighbor could improve.

What luck they have a neighbor of our kind,
  while we must suffer with  the other kind.

# VERSE THAT SPRINGS IN VERNAL

When 'neath an azure sky, dotted with fleecy clouds, a gentle balmy April zephyr heralds the awakening of the Goddess of Green: Spring.

Then midst the faithful tree, standing like sentinels of tender blades of grass, burgeoning buds begin to swell and blossom in the warm breeze, and violets peek through the land as birds on wing warble their bird-song.

This is a time of hope of birthing and re-birthing, fresh as the morning dew; a Garden of Eden, a springtime of desire to the young at heart; a new first love.

And from the now plowed fields come the gifts of Mother Nature and Poets: CORN!

# BILL

Bill was just a lad
  When he entered old N U
To learn to use a slide rule
  As he'd always wanted to.

Then he served his country as a lad
  In a manner picturesque.
He was skipper of an LSD,
  Which is a large steel desk.

Bill was yet a lad
  When his company became
A Wheeling corporate giant
  Of everlasting fame.

And as a lad his family grew
  Into a minor throng.
There was Bradley, Christy, then a "gap;"
  And Cathy came along.

Today Bill will be fifty,
  And we indeed are glad
That at half way to one hundred,
  Bill is still a lad.

# WINTER EMPATHY

A first frost lies quietly upon the northland,
awaiting marching orders from an angry wind.

Leaves tremble and fall, stripped of their blazing
colors and will to live.

A fish jumps, a deer drinks in a pond
for the last time till spring; perhaps forever.

No one sees the beauty, for winter is hard.  No
one smiles, nor do I;

My car won't start.

# FALLING DOWN

It was a little messy,
  And it seemed a little sad
But when Harry hit the sidewalk,
  Most of us were glad.

He walked up to the window,
  And stepped out on the ledge;
He waved good-bye to someone,
  Then jumped right off the edge.

His body fell quite quickly,
  Though to him it seemed so slow
For it gave him time to ponder,
  Where he would surely go.

For he'd really been a stinker,
  And he'd helped no one at all;
So there'd be not a soul out there
  To mourn his fatal fall.

But a crowd, indeed, had gathered
  To watch his final flight,
For he'd told us all about it
  In the paper last night.

*cont.*

He'd said that he was sorry,
  And had a debt to pay;
And we could watch him pay it,
  If we came downtown next day.

So from the highest building
  In our quiet town,
A thousand people watched and saw
  Poor Harry coming down.

Time passed so much more quickly
  As he reached the second floor.
He heard the cheers below him say,
  "Olé!  Harry's here no more!"

His altitude was zero
  When at last he changed his mind.
This thing that he was doing now,
  For him was much too kind.

He reached back for his wallet,
  And he sought someone to buy.
He'd offer twenty dollars now
  If just he needn't die.

For to bribe was still his nature,
  As we heard that awful "SPLAT,"
But he was short on time just then
  So finally that was that.

# SALUTATION

Within ten thousand silos,
  Ten thousand missiles lie,
Aimed to rain destruction
  From an unsuspecting sky.

Known to be in daily bread,
  Insidious in stealth,
Everything we eat and drink
  Is hazardous to health.

Housed within the air of life,
  Borne by every breeze,
Too small to see, too great to count,
  Are germs of all disease.

These observations come to mind
  When I hear someone say
Those worn-out words, so often heard
  "Have a nice day."

# TRAFFIC TO LOVE BY

I do enjoy a traffic jam, the excitement and the
peace; the squealing tires, the honking horns, the
fresh new epithets.  For as the world moves
swiftly by, here it is at rest.

Much unlike the others who populate this road;
I do not care the dinner's cold, the curtain's up
the game's begun or my appointment was at ten.

So when the heavens spill some snow or
drip a drop of rain, I slow my slow expressway
pace to help the traffic jam.  If there appear
construction signs, I slow down even more, as
I do for accidents that happened long ago.

I'm not the most loved driver who drives the
freeway lanes, but I'm at peace within myself,
I love a traffic jam.

## TO A HOT DOG MOM
## AT LITTLE LEAGUE PARK

Remember with the hot dogs,
  It's not the way one serves it,
It's more important that it go
  To the one who most deserves it.

Remember with the money,
  To count out every penny,
And if the kid ain't got enough,
  Be sure he don't get any.

# UNDER/SADDLE

A stinging spur, a jabbing bit,
  A crop on flank and braids.
He wondered if, in proper terms,
  He'd been put to the aids.

But patient with the rude request,
  He thought it best to trot;
And thus avoid the next of aids
  To come if he did not.

A sting, a jab he cantered on;
  A jab, now halt?  Reverse?
Perhaps it meant the same routine
  For better and for worse.

The class was done, the rider said,
  "I had him on the bit."
But that, straight from the horse's mouth,
  Was not the half of it.

# FOLLOW THE INSTRUCTIONS

Take the parts from the box,
  Handle them with care.
Match the round holes on the left
  Against those right and square.

Lean one side to 45,
  Insert a 1/8th bolt.
If it won't go, turn one turn,
  And give it half a jolt.

Do the same for each 1/8th,
  But not those marked 1/4th.
Those are for the other side,
  The side that faces North.

Find the piece marked "Do not bend,"
  And bend the strut a bit.
Put it on the part marked "A,"
  Or "X," if it won't fit.

On each bolt slide a ring,
  A washer and a nut.
Make it so each one of these
  Abut a nut and strut.

You're almost done, but next do this,
  Let your mind go wander,
For how you join "A" and "X,"
  You alone must ponder.

# ROUGHING IT

As I prepared the dinner meal,
  On my exotic range.
Lights and bells and thermostats
  Controlled each needed change.

I thought about the early days,
  And fires in open air,
With food cooked in a kindling smoke
  For taste beyond compare.

Yes, that is why there's charcoal rage,
  For barbecues each night,
And I succumbed, went outside,
  My charcoal to ignite.

It wouldn't flash, it wouldn't flare,
  I quickly was a learner,
And bought, installed, then quickly used,
  A two flame propane burner.

Then all was fine till winter time,
  When it got very cold.
I brought the grill inside the house,
  And now it can be told:

As I prepare the dinner meal
  On my exotic grill,
Lights and bells and thermostats
  Control each want and will.

# PILGRIM PROGRESS

This is a tale about a tale
  That was told in nursery school.
During story time one winter day,
  As was the common rule,

The teacher talked about our land
  And how it all began.
She read of Plymouth Rock,
  How Indians taught man

The ways to know just to survive
  Against a weather front.
And ways to know to cook their food,
  And ways to fish and hunt.

She read of how more Pilgrims came
  To make the freedom quest,
And how the natives were moved out,
  Further to the West.

When she was done with story time,
  She asked if anyone
Could retell what it meant,
  In the tale that she had spun.

cont.

And yes, there was one waving hand
  Who asked to tell the tale,
Just as the teacher had before;
  But not in each detail.

Billy stood and started out
  By telling of each ship,
And how they got to Plymouth Rock
  At the end of their long trip.

"They met the Indians," he said,
  "And then things got real bloody.
We told them once, and told them twice;
  'You'd better move it, buddy.' "

# UPSCALEDALE

The house on  the corner, without the
  three-car garage,
leaves outside a homeless non-BMW.
With inelegant design the place boasts not
  circlehead windows nor circular drive.
It is owned by a woman, over thirty,
  and a man who works, she  may too.
Perhaps they are married;  I don't know.
I've seen them at the mall, she not attired
  in breeches and boots;
  and he in a smoking jacket with utensils.
I can't say I know them; they are not at
  the club or at polo.
But I'm curious. Could they be poor?
Perhaps they didn't buy enough
  companies in the '80's.
I could ask someone,
  but that would not be neighborly in
  Upscaledale today.

# DIFFERENT KINDS OF CATS

A tough and roaring lion
  Met a gentle pussycat,
And thought at once of marriage
  And things that go with that.

While the cat at times seemed timid,
  She liked the lions style,
So sooner than you would have thought,
  They both walked down the aisle.

She said, "Of course I'll take him,
  For better or for worse,
For he's the grandest lion
  In this whole universe."

He said, "Of course I'll take her
  As long as we shall live,
For there is nothing she could do
  That I would not forgive."

So they started life together,
  And the lion was no louse;
The first thing that he did for her
  Was build a giant house.

She tried in turn to please him
  In every kind of way,
She cooked well in the kitchen;
  And you know what they say.

*cont.*

Then there were the kittens,
Together there were eight;
They raised them altogether
In a manner that was great.

At one time there was gossip
That said it wouldn't work,
That in a marriage such as this
A thousand dangers lurk.

I hope now all the doubters
Who said, "Hey, what's the hurry?"
Now wish them happiness and health
Each anniversary.

I paint for you this picture,
Though strange it seems at that,
Of a tough and roaring lion
And a gentle pussycat.

# BOARD MEETING

You take Big Burger,
  but Mini Machine is mine.
Bill can have half of Major Electric,
  if he pays me for Consolidated Oats.

Jack can have the banks if he agrees,
  no red tape on the loans.
Diamond Foods we all will share,
  and back it with our gold.

Forget the rails, let's go for air,
  and a shipping line.
Ma Bell has broken up,
  and we should get a piece or two.

Leave the autos to their own demise,
  we need some real estate;
Not much if it has oil below
  and condos up above.

It's time for lunch;
  let's grab a bite.
I'm a little short.
Could someone lend me "five?"

# JACKSON

There once was a family named Jackson,
Probably Anglo-Saxon
Who detested all wealth,
'Cept what they kept for themself;
And that which they didn't pay tax on.

The fellow, who's name was Jim,
Cared not what others called him.
He'd answer to James
Or various names,
But Jimmy did not really suit him.

And then there was Dame Eleanor,
Who certainly did know the score.
In a scheme to get rich,
She bred a fine bitch;
And now they have assets galore.

So you ask if I know the name Jackson.
I will now let you in on the facts, son.
Yes, of couse, I tell you,
I explained it to you
Though perhaps with a different syntax son.

## CHEF JACKIE

Forté is a certain strength,
  A special given gift.
With Jackie it's her cooking,
  A spiritual uplift.

For tea means at Jackie's
  Both tea and treats renowned.
Of course, some of the ladies come
  Just to look around.

'Fore T in the alphabet
  Comes letter S.
S is for this super chef-chef
  The best there is, I'd guess.

# DEAR ELIZABETH

You know it's very seldom
　That I ever give advice,
And mostly this is just because
　You are so very nice.

But since you're going off to school,
　And I cannot go too,
I have a few suggestions
　That I will give to you.

You'll meet some nifty people,
　And a rotter now and then,
But do remember it's not true
　That they are always men.

When classes start in early fall,
　You shouldn't miss too many,
Or else when grades are given out,
　You just might not get any.

And when it's time to take a test,
　Be sure you never cheat,
Unless there is a smart someone
　In an adjoining seat.

And never hide the cheat notes
　Where you might just get caught;
Hide them in a silly place
　Where no one would have thought.

*cont.*

And never copy papers
  That some other kid has writ,
Or you might copy words like "writ;"
  And they'd know you did it.

The best thing is to study hard,
  To live in the library
For all except the skiing months
  of March through February.

The weekends can be lots of fun,
  A blast if not a bomb;
 It gives you time to do such things
  As write to dad and mom.

Some kids may drink and do the things
  That kids now do today,
But don't be like them, it's not good;
  Your mother said to say.

I know the rules have changed a lot,
  Like who lives in the dorm;
And with long hair it's hard to tell
  The male from female form.

These are my thoughts on college days;
  I hope they will be yours.
And one more thing, at Christmas time,
  Please bring me home some Coors.

# MOVING MOUNTINGS

With reins in hand and hands in place
  On pommel and on mane,
Her foot turned out the stirrup iron;
  She bent her knee and  sprang.

But as she did the horse moved on,
  And she was up somewhere;
Not on the horse, nor at his side,
  But rather in midair.

Back down to earth she set the iron,
  And placed her foot within.
The horse moved; she hopped and sprang,
  And hopped and sprang again.

This time with luck, for she was up
  and mounted, whereupon
She reined a halt, then used her spurs
  but the horse would not move on.

# JOSÉ

Before José was thirty,
  He was clever, quick and bright.
No matter what the subject,
  His analysis was right.

He met and wed Diana,
  And said this lifetime shared,
Just proves the algorithm,
  $E = MC^2$.

Before José was forty,
  He was clever and was quick.
He found in error a theorem
  By a method that was slick.

With another formula,
  He'd created Myles and Joe.
Now the sum was greater than
  Its parts, or it seemed so.

Before José was fifty,
  As clever UPS guru,
He was Professor Hilarious,
  And lectured at old N U.

But now Jose is fifty,
  And has a Roto-Rooter need,
To check for foreign virus,
  Clear the channels and reseed.

# KAREN AND FRANK

This couple whose name was Corrado,
  For twenty-five years had a motto.
If you want to get rich,
  You must find a niche;
So they spent all their money on Lotto.

When Karen made ready the show,
  They had Kelly and Michael and Joe.
In discussing some more,
  Frank "got the door;"
She finally had to say, "whoa."

Frank, with words he was quick,
  But his poetry was not quite as slick.
He started a sonnet,
  But soon said, "Doggonit,
I'll ask Don for a good limerick."

# LIZZIE MCCOSKY

Lizzie McCosky, you may have heard,
Was here on the day her birthday occurred
For turkey and cake
And things ladies make;
What got stuffed was not just the  bird.

# CONNIE AND DON

Once upon a time
  A fellow had a twin.
Though not exactly like him,
  She was his next of kin.

She was a little younger,
  A minute, maybe two;
And just a little smarter,
  To show him what to do.

Well, she grew up and so did he;
  And both moved far away.
They married and had children,
  As married people may.

Later on their children
  Had some children too.
I guess this made them grandpamas
  From the children's point of view.

Today they have a birthday,
  And they are both just fine,
But wish they were together
  To toast the date with wine.

# CHRISTOPHER

He knew his mind, but didn't mind;
  And that was OK too;
His course was clear, he was sincere,
  He'd do what he would do.

He'd always had a flare for art,
  And a flare also for fish;
But what would be his lifelong choice?
  We did not know his wish.

Then he went on to get degrees
  Of kinds I'd never heard,
From east and west the sheepskins all
  Were graciously conferred.

But in the end who were his friends?
  His fishing friends, of course.
They helped him get a boat and crew,
  And were a money source.

So to catch some tons of fish he went
  To far Alaskan seas
With a doctorate in salmon
  And some liquid antifreeze.

This story's not completely told
  We'll let you know the rest.
About the salmon and the art
  And how he meets his quest.

# WILLIAM

When you're kind of down and out
'Cuz some chick's called you "Pop,"
And Colorback's brought out the gray
You thought that it would stop or:

When friends have asked how old you were,
And you've said, "Forty-nine,"
Then seen the little smiles that said
They didn't buy that line or:

When some kid not yet old enough
To buy a glass of beer,
Has told you how to do your job,
And he was right you fear or:

When you have sung or whistled tunes
Because your ankles crack,
But really worried more about
The pain up in your back or:

When someone's talked about the war,
And has meant Viet Nam,
But you thought just of World War II
And spoke about "The Bomb."

These are the times you need a lift,
Not booze, not drugs; I mean,
Like any man of fifty years,
You need a jelly bean.

# KAY AND BILL

There's nothing, some say, to making it through
  The first thirty years together;
But often, I've thought, it has more to do;
  With what is called, "What if" or "Whether."

What if it was that you hadn't been blessed
  With kids of the wonderful kind,
Who never caused heartache, never caused stress;
  And only gave you peace of mind.

Whether or not things could have gone wrong,
  And you'd had problems to face;
It's better, I think and you might agree
  That this was never the case.

What if, forbid, you two had a fight
  A fight you both had to win
And you'd found yourselves, as others have done,
  As much out of love as in.

Whether or not it is required,
  It's nice you had plenty of dough;
Not to bake, just to spend,
  It eases much stress as you know.

My visions, of course, are expressed from afar,
  And subject to errors of sight
But seeing you well and happy today
  Suggests that I may be right.

# POIME

Tom  Roby could never say poem,
So that it easily rhymed with home.
No, he had to say poime;
For which there's no rhoime,
But it shows us, indeed, his aplomb.

# FOOT FAULT
## (The gentle art of cleaning a horse's hoofs)

She pressed her shoulder in to his,
  A fore came off the ground.
She cradled it within her arms,
  And then he put it down.

She pressed once more, he shifted weight;
  Her pick was ready when,
Just when it seemed the foot would rise,
  He shifted back again.

In brief disgust she took a hind
  And gently drew it close.
But as she pushed it to the rear
  It came down on her toes.

Again she tried, his tail went "swoosh"
  And caught her in the face.
"What luck," she thought "it is to be
  Alone when in disgrace."

# POETIC DISSERTATION IN VERSE ON THE PROCLIVITY OF TOO SUPERFLUOUS AND RE-DUNDANT EUPHEMISTIC THOUGHT WITH REITERATION AND REPETITION OF SELF-OB-VIOUS AND SELF-EVIDENT FACTS

Make it clear.
Keep it short.
Write it well,
Then abort.

## About the Author

Don Cornwell was born and raised in Cedar Rapids, Iowa. He graduated from Northwestern University. Now retired (most of the time), he spent his business career in the computer field in marketing, training and writing positions. He still writes some computer "How to...." manuals, which keeps him in touch with the real world.

Don is past president of Poets Club of Chicago and Poets and Patrons. In recent years his light verse was published in *The Chronicle of the Horse*. He has also published a storybook poem *Horace the Pony* and You that is personalized for each young reader.